Third State of the Union Address

JAMES BUCHANAN

Published in 1859

TABLE OF CONTENTS

THIRD STATE OF THE UNION ADDRESS

THIRD STATE OF THE UNION ADDRESS

Fellow-Citizens of the Senate and House of Representatives:

Our deep and heartfelt gratitude is due to that Almighty Power which has bestowed upon us such varied and numerous blessings throughout the past year. The general health of the country has been excellent, our harvests have been unusually plentiful, and prosperity smiles throughout the land. Indeed, notwithstanding our demerits, we have much reason to believe from the past events in our history that we have enjoyed the special protection of Divine Providence ever since our origin as a nation. We have been exposed to many threatening and alarming difficulties in our progress, but on each successive occasion the impending cloud has been dissipated at the moment it appeared ready to burst upon our head, and the danger to our institutions has passed away. May we ever be under the divine guidance and protection. Whilst it is the duty of the President "from time to time to give to Congress information of the state of the Union," I shall not refer in detail to the recent sad and bloody occurrences at Harpers Ferry. Still, it is proper to observe that these events, however bad and cruel in themselves, derive their chief importance from the apprehension that they are but symptoms of an incurable disease in the public mind, which may break out in still more dangerous outrages and terminate at last in an open war by the North to abolish slavery in the South. Whilst for myself I entertain no such apprehension, they ought to afford a solemn warning to us all to beware of the approach of danger. Our Union is a stake of such inestimable value as to demand our constant and watchful vigilance for its preservation. In this view, let me implore my countrymen, North and South, to cultivate the ancient feelings of mutual forbearance and good will toward each other and strive to allay the demon spirit of sectional hatred and strife now alive in the land. This advice proceeds from the heart of an old public functionary whose service commenced in the last generation, among the wise and conservative statesmen of that day, now nearly all passed away, and whose first and dearest earthly wish is to leave his country tranquil, prosperous, united, and powerful.

We ought to reflect that in this age, and especially in this country, there is an incessant flux and reflux of public opinion. Questions which in their day assumed a most threatening aspect have now nearly gone from the memory of men. They are "volcanoes burnt out, and on the lava and ashes and squalid scoria of old eruptions grow the peaceful olive, the cheering vine, and the sustaining corn." Such, in my opinion, will prove to be the fate of the present sectional excitement should those who wisely seek to apply the remedy continue always to confine their efforts within the pale of the Constitution. If this course be pursued, the existing agitation on the subject of domestic slavery, like everything human, will have its day and give place to other and less threatening controversies. Public opinion in this country is all-powerful, and when it reaches a dangerous excess upon any question the good sense of the people will furnish the corrective and bring it back within safe limits. Still, to hasten this auspicious result at the present crisis we ought to remember that every rational creature must be presumed to intend the natural consequences of his own teachings. Those who announce abstract doctrines subversive of the Constitution and the Union must not be surprised should their heated partisans advance one step further and attempt by violence to carry these doctrines into practical effect. In this view of the subject, it ought never to be forgotten that however great may have been the political advantages resulting from the Union to every portion of our common country, these would all prove to be as nothing should the time ever arrive when they can not be enjoyed without serious danger to the personal safety of the people of fifteen members of the Confederacy. If the peace of the domestic fireside throughout these States should ever be invaded, if the mothers of families within this extensive region should not be able to retire to rest at night without suffering dreadful apprehensions of what may be their own fate and that of their children before the morning, it would be vain to recount to such a people the political benefits which result to them from the Union. Self-preservation is the first instinct of nature, and therefore any state of society in which the sword is all the time suspended over the heads of the people must at last become intolerable. But I indulge in no such gloomy forebodings. On the contrary, I firmly believe that the events at Harpers Ferry, by causing the people to pause and reflect upon the possible peril to their cherished institutions, will be the means under Providence of allaying the existing excitement and preventing further outbreaks of a similar character. They will resolve that the Constitution and the Union shall not be endangered by rash counsels, knowing that should "the silver cord be loosed or the golden bowl be broken at the fountain" human power could never reunite the scattered and hostile fragments.

I cordially congratulate you upon the final settlement by the Supreme Court of the United States of the question of slavery in the Territories, which had presented an aspect so truly formidable at the commencement of my Administration. The right has been established of every citizen to take his property of any kind, including slaves, into the common Territories belonging equally to all the States of the Confederacy, and to have it protected there under the Federal Constitution. Neither Congress nor a Territorial legislature nor any human power has any authority to annul or impair this vested right. The supreme judicial tribunal of the country, which is a coordinate branch of the Government, has sanctioned and affirmed these principles of constitutional law, so manifestly just in themselves and so well calculated to promote peace and harmony among the States. It is a striking proof of the sense of justice which is inherent in our people that the property in slaves has never been disturbed, to my knowledge, in any of the Territories. Even throughout the late troubles in Kansas there has not been any attempt, as I am credibly informed, to interfere in a single instance with the right of the master. Had any such attempt been made, the judiciary would doubtless have afforded an adequate remedy. Should they fail to do this hereafter, it will then be time enough to strengthen their hands by further legislation. Had it been decided that either Congress or the Territorial legislature possess the power to annul or impair the right to property in slaves, the evil would be intolerable. In the latter event there would be a struggle for a majority of the members of the legislature at each successive election, and the sacred rights of property held under the Federal Constitution would depend for the time being on the result. The agitation would thus be rendered incessant whilst the Territorial condition remained, and its baneful influence would keep alive a dangerous excitement among the people of the several States.

Thus has the status of a Territory during the intermediate period from its first settlement until it shall become a State been irrevocably fixed by the final decision of the Supreme Court. Fortunate has this been for the prosperity of the Territories, as well as the tranquillity of the States. Now emigrants from the North and the South, the East and the West, will meet in the Territories on a common platform, having brought with them that species of property best adapted, in their own opinion, to promote their welfare. From natural causes the slavery question will in each case soon virtually settle itself, and before the Territory is prepared for admission as a State into the Union this decision, one way or the other, will have been a foregone conclusion. Meanwhile the settlement of the new Territory will proceed without serious interruption, and its progress and prosperity will not be endangered or retarded by violent political struggles.

When in the progress of events the inhabitants of any Territory shall have reached the number required to form a State, they will then proceed in a regular manner and in the exercise of the rights of popular sovereignty to form a constitution preparatory to admission into the Union. After this has been done, to employ the language of the Kansas and Nebraska act, they "shall be received into the Union with or without slavery, as their constitution may prescribe at the time of their admission." This sound principle has happily been recognized in some form or other by an almost unanimous vote of both Houses of the last Congress.

All lawful means at my command have been employed, and shall continue to be employed, to execute the laws against the African slave trade. After a most careful and rigorous examination of our coasts and a thorough investigation of the subject, we have not been able to discover that any slaves have been imported into the United States except the cargo by the Wanderer, numbering between three and four hundred. Those engaged in this unlawful enterprise have been rigorously prosecuted, but not with as much success as their crimes have deserved. A number of them are still under prosecution.

Our history proves that the fathers of the Republic, in advance of all other nations, condemned the African slave trade. It was, notwithstanding, deemed expedient by the framers of the Constitution to deprive Congress of the power to prohibit "the migration or importation of such persons as any of the States now existing shall think proper to admit" "prior to the year 1808." It will be seen that this restriction on the power of Congress was confined to such States only as might think proper to admit the importation of slaves. It did not extend to other States or to the trade carried on abroad. Accordingly, we find that so early as the 22d March, 1794, Congress passed an act imposing severe penalties and punishments upon citizens and residents of the United States who should engage in this trade between foreign nations. The provisions of this act were extended and enforced by the act of 10th May, 1800.

Again, the States themselves had a clear right to waive the constitutional privilege intended for their benefit, and to prohibit by their own laws this trade at any time they thought proper previous to 1808. Several of them exercised this right before that period, and among them some containing the greatest number of slaves. This gave to Congress the immediate power to act in regard to all such States, because they themselves had removed the constitutional barrier. Congress accordingly passed an act on 28th February, 1803, "to prevent the importation of certain persons into certain States where by the laws thereof their admission is prohibited." In this manner the importation of African slaves into the United States was to a great extent prohibited some years in advance of 1808.

As the year 1808 approached Congress determined not to suffer this trade to exist even for a single day after they had the power to abolish it. On the 2d of March, 1807, they passed an act, to take effect "from and after the 1st day of January, 1808," prohibiting the importation of African slaves into the United States. This was followed by subsequent acts of a similar character, to which I need not specially refer. Such were the principles and such the practice of our ancestors more than fifty years ago in regard to the African slave trade. It did not occur to the revered patriots who had been delegates to the Convention, and afterwards became members of Congress, that in passing these laws they had violated the Constitution which they had framed with so much care and deliberation. They supposed that to prohibit Congress in express terms from exercising a specified power before an appointed day necessarily involved the right to exercise this power after that day had arrived.

If this were not the case, the framers of the Constitution had expended much labor in vain. Had they imagined that Congress would possess no power to prohibit the trade either before or after 1808, they would not have taken so much care to protect the States against the exercise of this power before that period. Nay, more, they would not have attached such vast importance to this provision as to have excluded it from the possibility of future repeal or amendment, to which other portions of the Constitution were exposed. It would, then, have been wholly unnecessary to ingraft on the fifth article of the Constitution, prescribing the mode of its own future amendment, the proviso "that no amendment which may be made prior to the year 1808 shall in any manner affect" the provision in the Constitution securing to the States the right to admit the importation of African slaves previous to that period. According to the adverse construction, the clause itself, on which so much care and discussion had been employed by the members of the Convention, was an absolute nullity from the beginning, and all that has since been done under it a mere usurpation.

It was well and wise to confer this power on Congress, because had it been left to the States its efficient exercise would have been impossible. In that event any one State could have effectually continued the trade, not only for itself, but for all the other slave States, though never so much against their will. And why? Because African slaves, when once brought within the limits of any one State in accordance with its laws, can not practically be excluded from any State where slavery exists. And even if all the States had separately passed laws prohibiting the importation of slaves, these laws would have failed of effect for want of a naval force to capture the slavers and to guard the coast. Such a force no State can employ in time of peace without the consent of Congress.

These acts of Congress, it is believed, have, with very rare and insignificant exceptions, accomplished their purpose. For a period of more than half a century there has been no perceptible addition to the number of our domestic slaves. During this period their advancement in civilization has far surpassed that of any other portion of the African race. The light and the blessings of Christianity have been extended to them, and both their moral and physical condition has been greatly improved.

Reopen the trade and it would be difficult to determine whether the effect would be more deleterious on the interests of the master or on those of the native-born slave. Of the evils to the master, the one most to be dreaded would be the introduction of wild, heathen, and ignorant barbarians among the sober, orderly, and quiet slaves whose ancestors have been on the soil for several generations. This might tend to barbarize, demoralize, and exasperate the whole mass and produce most deplorable consequences.

The effect upon the existing slave would, if possible, be still more deplorable. At present he is treated with kindness and humanity. He is well fed, well clothed, and not overworked. His condition is incomparably better than that of the coolies which modern nations of high civilization have employed as a substitute for African slaves. Both the philanthropy and the self-interest of the master have combined to produce this humane result. But let this trade be reopened and what will be the effect? The same to a considerable extent as on a neighboring island, the only spot now on earth where the African slave trade is openly tolerated, and this in defiance of solemn treaties with a power abundantly able at any moment to enforce their execution. There the master, intent upon present gain, extorts from the slave as much labor as his physical powers are capable of enduring, knowing that when death comes to his relief his place can be supplied at a price reduced to the lowest point by the competition of rival African slave traders. Should this ever be the case in our country, which I do not deem possible, the present useful character of the domestic institution, wherein those too old and too young to work are provided for with care and humanity and those capable of labor are not overtasked, would undergo an unfortunate change. The feeling of reciprocal dependence and attachment which now exists between master and slave would be converted into mutual distrust and hostility.

But we are obliged as a Christian and moral nation to consider what would be the effect upon unhappy Africa itself if we should reopen the slave trade. This would give the trade an impulse and extension which it has never had, even in its palmiest days. The numerous victims required to supply it would convert the whole slave coast into a perfect pandemonium, for which this country would be held responsible in the eyes both of God and man. Its petty tribes would then be constantly engaged in predatory wars against each other for the purpose of seizing slaves to supply the American market.

All hopes of African civilization would thus be ended.

On the other hand, when a market for African slaves shall no longer be furnished in Cuba, and thus all the world be closed against this trade,we may then indulge a reasonable hope for the gradual improvement of Africa. The chief motive of war among the tribes will cease whenever there is no longer any demand for slaves. The resources of that fertile but miserable country might then be developed by the hand of industry and afford subjects for legitimate foreign and domestic commerce. In this manner Christianity and civilization may gradually penetrate the existing gloom.

The wisdom of the course pursued by this Government toward China has been vindicated by the event. Whilst we sustained a neutral position in the war waged by Great Britain and France against the Chinese Empire, our late minister, in obedience to his instructions, judiciously cooperated with the ministers of these powers in all peaceful measures to secure by treaty the just concessions demanded by the interests of foreign commerce. The result is that satisfactory treaties have been concluded with China by the respective ministers of the United States, Great Britain, France, and Russia. Our "treaty, or general convention, of peace, amity, and commerce" with that Empire was concluded at Tien-tsin on the 18th June, 1858, and was ratified by the President, by and with the advice and consent of the Senate, on the 21st December following. On the 15th December, 1858, John E. Ward, a distinguished citizen of Georgia, was duly commissioned as envoy extraordinary and minister plenipotentiary to China.

He left the United States for the place of his destination on the 5th of February, 1859, bearing with him the ratified copy of this treaty, and arrived at Shanghai on the 28th May. From thence he proceeded to Peking on the 16th June, but did not arrive in that city until the 27th July. According to the terms of the treaty, the ratifications were to be exchanged on or before the 18th June, 1859. This was rendered impossible by reasons and events beyond his control, not necessary to detail; but still it is due to the Chinese authorities at Shanghai to state that they always assured him no advantage should be taken of the delay, and this pledge has been faithfully redeemed.

On the arrival of Mr. Ward at Peking he requested an audience of the Emperor to present his letter of credence. This he did not obtain, in consequence of his very proper refusal to submit to the humiliating ceremonies required by the etiquette of this strange people in approaching their sovereign. Nevertheless, the interviews on this question were conducted in the most friendly spirit and with all due regard to his personal feelings and the honor of his country. When a presentation to His Majesty was found to be impossible, the letter of credence from the President was received with peculiar honors by Kweiliang, "the Emperor's prime minister and the second man in the Empire to the Emperor himself." The ratifications of the treaty were afterwards, on the 16th of August, exchanged in proper form at Peit-sang. As the exchange did not take place until after the day prescribed by the treaty, it is deemed proper before its publication again to submit it to the Senate. It is but simple justice to the Chinese authorities to observe that throughout the whole transaction they appear to have acted in good faith and in a friendly spirit toward the United States. It is true this has been done after their own peculiar fashion; but we ought to regard with a lenient eye the ancient customs of an empire dating back for thousands of years, so far as this may be consistent with our own national honor. The conduct of our minister on the occasion has received my entire approbation.

In order to carry out the spirit of this treaty and to give it full effect it became necessary to conclude two supplemental conventions, the one for the adjustment and satisfaction of the claims of our citizens and the other to fix the tariff on imports and exports and to regulate the transit duties and trade of our merchants with China. This duty was satisfactorily performed by our late minister. These conventions bear date at Shanghai on the 8th November, 1858. Having been considered in the light of binding agreements subsidiary to the principal treaty, and to be carried into execution without delay, they do not provide for any formal ratification or exchange of ratifications by the contracting parties. This was not deemed necessary by the Chinese, who are already proceeding in good faith to satisfy the claims of our citizens and, it is hoped, to carry out the other provisions of the conventions. Still, I thought it was proper to submit them to the Senate by which they were ratified on the 3d of March, 1859. The ratified copies, however, did not reach Shanghai until after the departure of our minister to Peking, and these conventions could not, therefore, be exchanged at the same time with the principal treaty. No doubt is entertained that they will be ratified and exchanged by the Chinese Government should this be thought advisable; but under the circumstances presented I shall consider them binding engagements from their date on both parties, and cause them to be published as such for the information and guidance of our merchants trading with the Chinese Empire.

It affords me much satisfaction to inform you that all our difficulties with the Republic of Paraguay have been satisfactorily adjusted. It happily did not become necessary to employ the force for this purpose which Congress had placed at my command under the joint resolution of 2d June, 1858. On the contrary, the President of that Republic, in a friendly spirit, acceded promptly to the just and reasonable demands of the Government of the United States. Our commissioner arrived at Assumption, the capital of the Republic, on the 25th of January, 1859, and left it on the 17th of February, having in three weeks ably and successfully accomplished all the objects of his mission. The treaties which he has concluded will be immediately submitted to the Senate.

In the view that the employment of other than peaceful means might become necessary to obtain "just satisfaction" from Paraguay, a strong naval force was concentrated in the waters of the La Plata to await contingencies whilst our commissioner ascended the rivers to Assumption. The Navy Department is entitled to great credit for the promptness, efficiency, and economy with which this expedition was fitted out and conducted. It consisted of 19 armed vessels, great and small, carrying 200 guns and 2,500 men, all under the command of the veteran and gallant Shubrick. The entire expenses of the expedition have been defrayed out of the ordinary appropriations for the naval service, except the sum of $289,000, applied to the purchase of seven of the steamers constituting a part of it, under the authority of the naval appropriation act of the 3d March last. It is believed that these steamers are worth more than their cost, and they are all now usefully and actively employed in the naval service.

The appearance of so large a force, fitted out in such a prompt manner, in the far-distant waters of the La Plata, and the admirable conduct of the officers and men employed in it, have had a happy effect in favor of our country throughout all that remote portion of the world. Our relations with the great Empires of France and Russia, as well as with all other governments on the continent of Europe, unless we may except that of Spain, happily continue to be of the most friendly character. In my last annual message I presented a statement of the unsatisfactory condition of our relations with Spain, and I regret to say that this has not materially improved.

Without special reference to other claims, even the "Cuban claims," the payment of which has been ably urged by our ministers, and in which more than a hundred of our citizens are directly interested, remain unsatisfied, notwithstanding both their justice and their amount ($128,635.54) had been recognized and ascertained by the Spanish Government itself.

I again recommend that an appropriation be made "to be paid to the Spanish Government for the purpose of distribution among the claimants in the Amistad case." In common with two of my predecessors, I entertain no doubt that this is required by our treaty with Spain of the 27th October, 1795. The failure to discharge this obligation has been employed by the cabinet of Madrid as a reason against the settlement of our claims.

I need not repeat the arguments which I urged in my last annual message in favor of the acquisition of Cuba by fair purchase. My opinions on that measure remain unchanged. I therefore again invite the serious attention of Congress to this important subject. Without a recognition of this policy on their part it will be almost impossible to institute negotiations with any reasonable prospect of success. Until a recent period there was good reason to believe that I should be able to announce to you on the present occasion that our difficulties with Great Britain arising out of the Clayton and Bulwer treaty had been finally adjusted in a manner alike honorable and satisfactory to both parties. From causes, however, which the British Government had not anticipated, they have not yet completed treaty arrangements with the Republics of Honduras and Nicaragua, in pursuance of the understanding between the two Governments. It is, nevertheless, confidently expected that this good work will ere long be accomplished.

Whilst indulging the hope that no other subject remained which could disturb the good understanding between the two countries, the question arising out of the adverse claims of the parties to the island of San Juan, under the Oregon treaty of the 15th June, 1846, suddenly assumed a threatening prominence. In order to prevent unfortunate collisions on that remote frontier, the late Secretary of State, on the 17th July, 1855, addressed a note to Mr. Crampton, then British minister at Washington, communicating to him a copy of the instructions which he (Mr. Marcy) had given on the 14th July to Governor Stevens, of Washington Territory, having a special reference to an "apprehended conflict between our citizens and the British subjects on the island of San Juan." To prevent this the governor was instructed "that the officers of the Territory should abstain from all acts on the disputed grounds which are calculated to provoke any conflicts, so far as it can be done without implying the concession to the authorities of Great Britain of an exclusive right over the premises. The title ought to be settled before either party should attempt to exclude the other by force or exercise complete and exclusive sovereign rights within the fairly disputed limits." In acknowledging the receipt on the next day of Mr. Marcy's note the British minister expressed his entire concurrence "in the propriety of the course recommended to the governor of Washington Territory by your [Mr. Marcy's] instructions to that officer," and stating that he had "lost no time in transmitting a copy of that document to the Governor-General of British North America" and had "earnestly recommended to His Excellency to take such measures as to him may appear best calculated to secure on the part of the British local authorities and the inhabitants of the neighborhood of the line in question the exercise of the same spirit of forbearance which is inculcated by you [Mr. Marcy] on the authorities and citizens of the United States."

Thus matters remained upon the faith of this arrangement until the 9th July last, when General Harney paid a visit to the island. He found upon it twenty-five American residents with their families, and also an establishment of the Hudsons Bay Company for the purpose of raising sheep. A short time before his arrival one of these residents had shot an animal belonging to the company whilst trespassing upon his premises, for which, however, he offered to pay twice its value, but that was refused. Soon after "the chief factor of the company at Victoria, Mr. Dalles, son-in-law of Governor Douglas, came to the island in the British sloop of war

Satellite and threatened to take this American [Mr. Cutler] by force to Victoria to answer for the trespass he had committed. The American seized his rifle and told Mr. Dalles if any such attempt was made he would kill him upon the spot. The affair then ended."

Under these circumstances the American settlers presented a petition to the General "through the United States inspector of customs, Mr. Hubbs, to place a force upon the island to protect them from the Indians as well as the oppressive interference of the authorities of the Hudsons Bay Company at Victoria with their rights as American citizens." The General immediately responded to this petition, and ordered Captain George E. Pickett, Ninth Infantry, "to establish his company on Bellevue, or San Juan Island, on some suitable position near the harbor at the southeastern extremity." This order was promptly obeyed and a military post was established at the place designated. The force was afterwards increased, so that by the last return the whole number of troops then on the island amounted in the aggregate to 691 men.

Whilst I do not deem it proper on the present occasion to go further into the subject and discuss the weight which ought to be attached to the statements of the British colonial authorities contesting the accuracy of the information on which the gallant General acted, it was due to him that I should thus present his own reasons for issuing the order to Captain Pickett. From these it is quite clear his object was to prevent the British authorities on Vancouvers Island from exercising jurisdiction over American residents on the island of San Juan, as well as to protect them against the incursions of the Indians. Much excitement prevailed for some time throughout that region, and serious danger of collision between the parties was apprehended. The British had a large naval force in the vicinity, and it is but an act of simple justice to the admiral on that station to state that he wisely and discreetly forbore to commit any hostile act, but determined to refer the whole affair to his Government and await their instructions.

This aspect of the matter, in my opinion, demanded serious attention. It would have been a great calamity for both nations had they been precipitated into acts of hostility, not on the question of title to the island, but merely concerning what should be its condition during the intervening period whilst the two Governments might be employed in settling the question to which of them it belongs. For this reason Lieutenant-General Scott was dispatched, on the 17th of September last, to Washington Territory to take immediate command of the United States forces on the Pacific Coast, should he deem this necessary. The main object of his mission was to carry out the spirit of the precautionary arrangement between the late Secretary of State and the British minister, and thus to preserve the peace and prevent collision between the British and American authorities pending the negotiations between the two Governments. Entertaining no doubt of the validity of our title, I need scarcely add that in any event American citizens were to be placed on a footing at least as favorable as that of British subjects, it being understood that Captain Pickett's company should remain on the island. It is proper to observe that, considering the distance from the scene of action and in ignorance of what might have transpired on the spot before the General's arrival, it was necessary to leave much to his discretion; and I am happy to state the event has proven that this discretion could not have been intrusted to more competent hands. General Scott has recently returned from his mission, having successfully accomplished its objects, and there is no longer any good reason to apprehend a collision between the forces of the two countries during the pendency of the existing negotiations. I regret to inform you that there has been no improvement in the affairs of Mexico since my last annual message, and I am again obliged to ask the earnest attention of Congress to the unhappy condition of that Republic.

The constituent Congress of Mexico, which adjourned on the 17th February, 1857, adopted a constitution and provided for a popular election. This took place in the following July (1857), and General Comonfort was chosen President almost without opposition. At the same election a new Congress was chosen, whose first session commenced on the 16th of September (1857). By the constitution of 1857 the Presidential term was to begin on the 1st of December (1857) and continue for four years. On that day General Comonfort appeared before the assembled Congress in the City of Mexico, took the oath to support the new constitution, and was duly inaugurated as President. Within a month afterwards he had been driven from the capital and a military rebellion had assigned the supreme power of the Republic to General Zuloaga. The constitution provided that in the absence of the President his office should devolve upon the chief justice of the supreme court; and General Comonfort having left the country, this functionary, General Juarez, proceeded to form at Guanajuato a constitutional Government. Before this was officially known, however, at the capital the Government of Zuloaga had been recognized by the entire diplomatic corps, including the minister of the United States, as the de facto Government of Mexico. The constitutional President, nevertheless, maintained his position with firmness, and was soon established, with his cabinet, at Vera Cruz. Meanwhile the Government of Zuloaga was earnestly resisted in many parts of the Republic, and even in the capital, a portion of the army having pronounced against it, its functions were declared terminated, and an assembly of citizens was invited for the choice of a new President. This assembly elected General Miramort, but that officer repudiated the plan under which he was chosen, and Zuloaga was thus restored to his previous position. He assumed it, however, only to withdraw from it; and Miramon, having become by his appointment "President substitute," continues with that title at the head of the insurgent party.

In my last annual message I communicated to Congress the circumstances under which the late minister of the United States suspended his official relations with the central Government and withdrew from the country. It was impossible to maintain friendly intercourse with a government like that at the capital, under whose usurped authority wrongs were constantly committed, but never redressed. Had this been an established government, with its power extending by the consent of the people over the whole of Mexico, a resort to hostilities against it would have been quite justifiable, and, indeed, necessary. But the country was a prey to civil war, and it was hoped that the success of the constitutional President might lead to a condition of things less injurious to the United States. This success became so probable that in January last I employed a reliable agent to visit Mexico and report to me the actual condition and prospects of the contending parties. In consequence of his report and from information which reached me from other sources favorable to the prospects of the constitutional cause, I felt justified in appointing a new minister to Mexico, who might embrace the earliest suitable opportunity of restoring our diplomatic relations with that Republic. For this purpose a distinguished citizen of Maryland was selected, who proceeded on his mission on the 8th of March last, with discretionary authority to recognize the Government of President Juarez if on his arrival in Mexico he should find it entitled to such recognition according to the established practice of the United States.

On the 7th of April following Mr. McLane presented his credentials to President Juarez, having no hesitation "in pronouncing the Government of Juarez to be the only existing government of the Republic." He was cordially received by the authorities at Vera Cruz, and they have ever since manifested the most friendly disposition toward the United States.

Unhappily, however, the constitutional Government has not been able to establish its power over the whole Republic. It is supported by a large majority of the people and the States, but there are important parts of the country where it can enforce no obedience.

General Miramon maintains himself at the capital, and in some of the distant Provinces there are military governors who pay little respect to the decrees of either Government. In the meantime the excesses which always attend upon civil war, especially in Mexico, are constantly recurring. Outrages of the worst description are committed both upon persons and property. There is scarcely any form of injury which has not been suffered by our citizens in Mexico during the last few years. We have been nominally at peace with that Republic, but "so far as the interests of our commerce, or of our citizens who have visited the country as merchants, shipmasters, or in other capacities, are concerned, we might as well have been at war." Life has been insecure, property unprotected, and trade impossible except at a risk of loss which prudent men can not be expected to incur. Important contracts, involving large expenditures, entered into by the central Government, have been set at defiance by the local governments. Peaceful American residents, occupying their rightful possessions, have been suddenly expelled the country, in defiance of treaties and by the mere force of arbitrary power. Even the course of justice has not been safe from control, and a recent decree of Miramort permits the intervention of Government in all suits where either party is a foreigner. Vessels of the United States have been seized without law, and a consular officer who protested against such seizure has been fined and imprisoned for disrespect to the authorities. Military contributions have been levied in violation of every principle of right, and the American who resisted the lawless demand has had his property forcibly taken away and has been himself banished. From a conflict of authority in different parts of the country tariff duties which have been paid in one place have been exacted over again in another place. Large numbers of our citizens have been arrested and imprisoned without any form of examination or any opportunity for a hearing, and even when released have only obtained their liberty after much suffering and injury, and without any hope of redress. The wholesale massacre of Crabbe and his associates without trial in Sonora, as well as the seizure and murder of four sick Americans who had taken shelter in the house of an American upon the soil of the United States, was communicated to Congress at its last session. Murders of a still more atrocious character have been committed in the very heart of Mexico, under the authority of Miramon's Government, during the present year. Some of these were only worthy of a barbarous age, and if they had not been dearly proven would have seemed impossible in a country which claims to be civilized. Of this description was the brutal massacre in April last, by order of General Marquez, of three American physicians who were seized in the hospital at Tacubaya while attending upon the sick and the dying of both parties, and without trial, as without crime, were hurried away to speedy execution. Little less shocking was the recent fate of Ormond Chase, who was shot in Tepic on the 7th of August by order of the same Mexican general, not only without a trial, but without any conjecture by his friends of the cause of his arrest. He is represented as a young man of good character and intelligence, who had made numerous friends in Tepic by the courage and humanity which he had displayed on several trying occasions; and his death was as unexpected as it was shocking to the whole community. Other outrages might be enumerated, but these are sufficient to illustrate the wretched state of the country and the unprotected condition of the persons and property of our citizens in Mexico.

In all these cases our ministers have been constant and faithful in their demands for redress, but both they and this Government, which they have successively represented, have been wholly powerless to make their demands effective. Their testimony in this respect and in reference to the only remedy which in their judgments would meet the exigency has been both uniform and emphatic. "Nothing but a manifestation of the power of the Government of the United States," wrote our late minister in 1856, "and of its purpose to punish these wrongs will avail. I assure you that the universal belief here is that there is nothing to be apprehended from the Government of the United States, and that local Mexican officials can commit these outrages upon American citizens with absolute impunity." "I hope the President," wrote our present minister in August last, "will feel authorized to ask from Congress the power to enter Mexico with the military forces of the United States at the call of the constitutional authorities, in order to protect the citizens and the treaty rights of the United States. Unless such a power is conferred upon him, neither the one nor the other will be respected in the existing state of anarchy and disorder, and the outrages already perpetrated will never be chastised; and, as I assured you in my No. 23, all these evils must increase until every vestige of order and government disappears from the country." I have been reluctantly led to the same opinion, and in justice to my countrymen who have suffered wrongs from Mexico and who may still suffer them I feel bound to announce this conclusion to Congress.

The case presented, however, is not merely a case of individual claims, although our just claims against Mexico have reached a very large amount; nor is it merely the case of protection to the lives and property of the few Americans who may still remain in Mexico, although the life and property of every American citizen ought to be sacredly protected in every quarter of the world; but it is a question which relates to the future as well as to the present and the past, and which involves, indirectly at least, the whole subject of our duty to Mexico as a neighboring State. The exercise of the power of the United States in that country to redress the wrongs and protect the rights of our own citizens is none the less to be desired because efficient and necessary aid may thus be rendered at the same time to restore peace and order to Mexico itself. In the accomplishment of this result the people of the United States must necessarily feel a deep and earnest interest. Mexico ought to be a rich and prosperous and powerful Republic. She possesses an extensive territory, a fertile soil, and an incalculable store of mineral wealth. She occupies an important position between the Gulf and the ocean for transit routes and for commerce. Is it possible that such a country as this can be given up to anarchy and ruin without an effort from any quarter for its rescue and its safety? Will the commercial nations of the world, which have so many interests connected with it, remain wholly indifferent to such a result? Can the United States especially, which ought to share most largely in its commercial intercourse, allow their immediate neighbor thus to destroy itself and injure them? Yet without support from some quarter it is impossible to perceive how Mexico can resume her position among nations and enter upon a career which promises any good results. The aid which she requires, and which the interests of all commercial countries require that she should have, it belongs to this Government to render, not only by virtue of our neighborhood to Mexico, along whose territory we have a continuous frontier of nearly a thousand miles, but by virtue also of our established policy, which is inconsistent with the intervention of any European power in the domestic concerns of that Republic.

The wrongs which we have suffered from Mexico are before the world and must deeply impress every American citizen. A government which is either unable or unwilling to redress such wrongs is derelict to its highest duties. The difficulty consists in selecting and enforcing the remedy. We may in vain apply to the constitutional Government at Vera Cruz, although it is well disposed to do us justice, for adequate redress. Whilst its authority is acknowledged in all the important ports and throughout the seacoasts of the Republic, its power does not extend to the City of Mexico and the States in its vicinity, where nearly all the recent outrages have been committed on American citizens. We must penetrate into the interior before we can reach the offenders, and this can only be done by passing through the territory in the occupation of the constitutional Government. The most acceptable and least difficult mode of accomplishing the object will be to act in concert with that Government. Their consent and their aid might, I believe, be obtained; but if not, our obligation to protect our own citizens in their just rights secured by treaty would not be the less imperative. For these reasons I recommend to Congress to pass a law authorizing the President under such conditions as they may deem expedient, to employ a sufficient military force to enter Mexico for the purpose of obtaining indemnity for the past and security for the future. I purposely refrain from any suggestion as to whether this force shall consist of regular troops or volunteers, or both. This question may be most appropriately left to the decision of Congress. I would merely observe that should volunteers be selected such a force could be easily raised in this country among those who sympathize with the sufferings of our unfortunate fellow-citizens in Mexico and with the unhappy condition of that Republic. Such an accession to the forces of the constitutional Government would enable it soon to reach the City of Mexico and extend its power over the whole Republic. In that event there is no reason to doubt that the just claims of our citizens would be satisfied and adequate redress obtained for the injuries inflicted upon them. The constitutional Government have ever evinced a strong desire to do justice, and this might be secured in advance by a preliminary treaty.

It may be said that these measures will, at least indirectly, be inconsistent with our wise and settled policy not to interfere in the domestic concerns of foreign nations. But does not the present case fairly constitute an exception? An adjoining Republic is in a state of anarchy and confusion from which she has proved wholly unable to extricate herself. She is entirely destitute of the power to maintain peace upon her borders or to prevent the incursions of banditti into our territory. In her fate and in her fortune, in her power to establish and maintain a settled government, we have a far deeper interest, socially, commercially, and politically, than any other nation. She is now a wreck upon the ocean, drifting about as she is impelled by different factions. As a good neighbor, shall we not extend to her a helping hand to save her? If we do not, it would not be surprising should some other nation undertake the task, and thus force us to interfere at last, under circumstances of increased difficulty, for the maintenance of our established policy.

I repeat the recommendation contained in my last annual message that authority may be given to the President to establish one or more temporary military posts across the Mexican line in Sonora and Chihuahua, where these may be necessary to protect the lives and property of American and Mexican citizens against the incursions and depredations of the Indians, as well as of lawless rovers, on that remote region. The establishment of one such post at a point called Arispe, in Sonora, in a country now almost depopulated by the hostile inroads of the Indians from our side of the line, would, it is believed, have prevented much injury and many cruelties during the past season. A state of lawlessness and violence prevails on that distant frontier. Life and property are there wholly insecure. The population of Arizona, now numbering more than 10,000 souls, are practically destitute of government, of laws, or of any regular administration of justice. Murder, rapine, and other crimes are committed with impunity. I therefore again call the attention of Congress to the necessity for establishing a Territorial government over Arizona.

The treaty with Nicaragua of the 16th of February, 1857, to which I referred in my last annual message, failed to receive the ratification of the Government of that Republic, for reasons which I need not enumerate. A similar treaty has been since concluded between the parties, bearing date on the 16th March, 1859, which has already been ratified by the Nicaraguan Congress. This will be immediately submitted to the Senate for their ratification. Its provisions can not, I think, fail to be acceptable to the people of both countries.

Our claims against the Governments of Costa Rica and Nicaragua remain unredressed, though they are pressed in an earnest manner and not without hope of success.

I deem it to be my duty once more earnestly to recommend to Congress the passage of a law authorizing the President to employ the naval force at his command for the purpose of protecting the lives and property of American citizens passing in transit across the Panama, Nicaragua, and Tehuantepec routes against sudden and lawless outbreaks and depredations. I shall not repeat the arguments employed in former messages in support of this measure. Suffice it to say that the lives of many of our people and the security of vast amounts of treasure passing and repassing over one or more of these routes between the Atlantic and Pacific may be deeply involved in the action of Congress on this subject.

I would also again recommend to Congress that authority be given to the President to employ the naval force to protect American merchant vessels, their crews and cargoes, against violent and lawless seizure and confiscation in the ports of Mexico and the Spanish American States when these countries may be in a disturbed and revolutionary condition. The mere knowledge that such an authority had been conferred, as I have already stated, would of itself in a great degree prevent the evil. Neither would this require any additional appropriation for the naval service.

The chief objection urged against the grant of this authority is that Congress by conferring it would violate the Constitution; that it would be a transfer of the war-making, or, strictly speaking, the war-declaring, power to the Executive. If this were well rounded, it would, of course, be conclusive. A very brief examination, however, will place this objection at rest.

Congress possess the sole and exclusive power under the Constitution "to declare war." They alone can "raise and support armies" and "provide and maintain a navy." But after Congress shall have declared war and provided the force necessary to carry it on the President, as Commander in Chief of the Army and Navy, can alone employ this force in making war against the enemy. This is the plain language, and history proves that it was the well-known intention of the framers, of the Constitution.

It will not be denied that the general "power to declare war" is without limitation and embraces within itself not only what writers on the law of nations term a public or perfect war, but also an imperfect war, and, in short, every species of hostility, however confined or limited. Without the authority of Congress the President can not fire a hostile gun in any case except to repel the attacks of an enemy. It will not be doubted that under this power Congress could, if they thought proper, authorize the President to employ the force at his command to seize a vessel belonging to an American citizen which had been illegally and unjustly captured in a foreign port and restore it to its owner. But can Congress only act after the fact, after the mischief has been done? Have they no power to confer upon the President the authority in advance to furnish instant redress should such a case afterwards occur? Must they wait until the mischief has been done, and can they apply the remedy only when it is too late? To confer this authority to meet future cases under circumstances strictly specified is as clearly within the war-declaring power as such an authority conferred upon the President by act of Congress after the deed had been done. In the progress of a great nation many exigencies must arise imperatively requiring that Congress should authorize the President to act promptly on certain conditions which may or may not afterwards arise. Our history has already presented a number of such cases. I shall refer only to the latest. Under the resolution of June 2, 1858, "for the adjustment of difficulties with the Republic of Paraguay," the President is "authorized to adopt such measures and use such force as in his judgment may be necessary and advisable in the event of a refusal of just satisfaction by the Government of Paraguay." "Just satisfaction" for what? For "the attack on the United States steamer Water Witch" and "other matters referred to in the annual message of the President." Here the power is expressly granted upon the condition that the Government of Paraguay shall refuse to render this "just satisfaction." In this and other similar cases Congress have conferred upon the President power in advance to employ the Army and Navy upon the happening of contingent future events; and this most certainly is embraced within the power to declare war.

Now, if this conditional and contingent power could be constitutionally conferred upon the President in the case of Paraguay, why may it not be conferred for the purpose of protecting the lives and property of American citizens in the event that they may be violently and unlawfully attacked in passing over the transit routes to and from California or assailed by the seizure of their vessels in a foreign port? To deny this power is to render the Navy in a great degree useless for the protection of the lives and property of American citizens in countries where neither protection nor redress can be otherwise obtained.

The Thirty-fifth Congress terminated on the 3d of March, 1859, without having passed the "act making appropriations for the service of the Post-Office Department during the fiscal year ending the 30th of June, 1860," This act also contained an appropriation "to supply deficiencies in the revenue of the Post-Office Department for the year ending 30th June, 1859." I believe this is the first instance since the origin of the Federal Government, now more than seventy years ago, when any Congress went out of existence without having passed all the general appropriation bills necessary to carry on the Government until the regular period for the meeting of a new Congress. This event imposed on the Executive a grave responsibility. It presented a choice of evils.

Had this omission of duty occurred at the first session of the last Congress, the remedy would have been plain. I might then have instantly recalled them to complete their work, and this without expense to the Government.

But on the 4th of March last there were fifteen of the thirty-three States which had not elected any Representatives to the present Congress. Had Congress been called together immediately, these States would have been virtually disfranchised. If an intermediate period had been selected, several of the States would have been compelled to hold extra sessions of their legislatures, at great inconvenience and expense, to provide for elections at an earlier day than that previously fixed by law. In the regular course ten of these States would not elect until after the beginning of August, and five of these ten not until October and November.

On the other hand, when I came to examine carefully the condition of the Post-Office Department, I did not meet as many or as great difficulties as I had apprehended. Had the bill which failed been confined to appropriations for the fiscal year ending on the 30th June next, there would have been no reason of pressing importance for the call of an extra session. Nothing would become due on contracts (those with railroad companies only excepted) for carrying the mail for the first quarter of the present fiscal year, commencing on the 1st of July, until the 1st of December-less than one week before the meeting of the present Congress. The reason is that the mail contractors for this and the current year did not complete their first quarter's service until the 30th September last, and by the terms of their contracts sixty days more are allowed for the settlement of their accounts before the Department could be called upon for payment.

The great difficulty and the great hardship consisted in the failure to provide for the payment of the deficiency in the fiscal year ending the 30th June, 1859. The Department had entered into contracts, in obedience to existing laws, for the service of that fiscal year, and the contractors were fairly entitled to their compensation as it became due. The deficiency as stated in the bill amounted to $3,838,728, but after a careful settlement of all these accounts it has been ascertained that it amounts to $4,296,009. With the scanty means at his command the Postmaster-General has managed to pay that portion of this deficiency which occurred in the first two quarters of the past fiscal year, ending on the 31st December last. In the meantime the contractors themselves, under these trying circumstances, have behaved in a manner worthy of all commendation. They had one resource in the midst of their embarrassments. After the amount due to each of them had been ascertained and finally settled according to law, this became a specific debt of record against the United States, which enabled them to borrow money on this unquestionable security. Still, they were obliged to pay interest in consequence of the default of Congress, and on every principle of justice ought to receive interest from the Government. This interest should commence from the date when a warrant would have issued for the payment of the principal had an appropriation been made for this purpose. Calculated up to the 1st December, it will not exceed $96,660-

a sum not to be taken into account when contrasted with the great difficulties and embarrassments of a public and private character, both to the people and the States, which would have resulted from convening and holding a special session of Congress. For these reasons I recommend the passage of a bill at as early a day as may be practicable to provide for the payment of the amount, with interest, due to these last-mentioned contractors, as well as to make the necessary appropriations for the service of the Post-Office Department for the current fiscal year.

The failure to pass the Post-Office bill necessarily gives birth to serious reflections. Congress, by refusing to pass the general appropriation bills necessary to carry on the Government, may not only arrest its action, but might even destroy its existence. The Army, the Navy, the judiciary, in short, every department of the Government, can no longer perform their functions if Congress refuse the money necessary for their support. If this failure should teach the country the necessity of electing a full Congress in sufficient time to enable the President to convene them in any emergency, even immediately after the old Congress has expired, it will have been productive of great good. In a time of sudden and alarming danger, foreign or domestic, which all nations must expect to encounter in their progress, the very salvation of our institutions may be staked upon the assembling of Congress without delay. If under such circumstances the President should find himself in the condition in which he was placed at the close of the last Congress, with nearly half the States of the Union destitute of representatives, the consequences might he disastrous. I therefore recommend to Congress to carry into effect the provisions of the Constitution on this subject, and to pass a law appointing some day previous to the 4th March in each year of odd number for the election of Representatives throughout all the States. They have already appointed a day for the election of electors for President and Vice-President, and this measure has been approved by the country.

I would again express a most decided opinion in favor of the construction of a Pacific railroad, for the reasons stated in my two last annual messages. When I reflect upon what would be the defenseless condition of our States and Territories west of the Rocky Mountains in case of a war with a naval power sufficiently strong to interrupt all intercourse with them by the routes across the Isthmus, I am still more convinced than ever of the vast importance of this railroad. I have never doubted the constitutional competency of Congress to provide for its construction, but this exclusively under the war-making power. Besides, the Constitution expressly requires as an imperative duty that "the United States shall protect each of them [the States] against invasion." I am at a loss to conceive how this protection can be afforded to California and Oregon against such a naval power by any other means. I repeat the opinion contained in my last annual message that it would be inexpedient for the Government to undertake this great work by agents of its own appointment and under its direct and exclusive control. This would increase the patronage of the Executive to a dangerous extent and would foster a system of jobbing and corruption which no vigilance on the part of Federal officials could prevent. The construction of this road ought, therefore, to be intrusted to incorporated companies or other agencies who would exercise that active and vigilant supervision over it which can be inspired alone by a sense of corporate and individual interest. I venture to assert that the additional cost of transporting troops, munitions of war, and necessary supplies for the Army across the vast intervening plains to our possessions on the Pacific Coast would be greater in such a war than the whole amount required to construct the road. And yet this resort would after all be inadequate for their defense and protection.

We have yet scarcely recovered from the habits of extravagant expenditure produced by our overflowing Treasury during several years prior to the commencement of my Administration. The financial reverses which we have since experienced ought to teach us all to scrutinize our expenditures with the greatest vigilance and to reduce them to the lowest possible point. The Executive Departments of the Government have devoted themselves to the accomplishment of this object with considerable success, as will appear from their different reports and estimates. To these I invite the scrutiny of Congress, for the purpose of reducing them still lower, if this be practicable consistent with the great public interests of the country. In aid of the policy of retrenchment, I pledge myself to examine closely the bills appropriating lands or money, so that if any of these should inadvertently pass both Houses, as must sometimes be the case, I may afford them an opportunity for reconsideration. At the same time, we ought never to forget that true public economy consists not in withholding the means necessary to accomplish important national objects confided to us by the Constitution, but in taking care that the money appropriated for these purposes shall be faithfully and frugally expended.

It will appear from the report of the Secretary of the Treasury that it is extremely doubtful, to say the least, whether we shall be able to pass through the present and the next fiscal year without providing additional revenue. This can only be accomplished by strictly confining the appropriations within the estimates of the different Departments, without making an allowance for any additional expenditures which Congress may think proper, in their discretion, to authorize, and without providing for the redemption of any portion of the $20,000,000 of Treasury notes which have been already issued. In the event of a deficiency, which I consider probable, this ought never to be supplied by a resort to additional loans. It would be a ruinous practice in the days of peace and prosperity to go on increasing the national debt to meet the ordinary expenses of the Government. This policy would cripple our resources and impair our credit in case the existence of war should render it necessary to borrow money. Should such a deficiency occur as I apprehend, I would recommend that the necessary revenue be raised by an increase of our present duties on imports. I need not repeat the opinions expressed in my last annual message as to the best mode and manner of accomplishing this object, and shall now merely observe that these have since undergone no change. The report of the Secretary of the Treasury will explain in detail the operations of that Department of the Government. The receipts into the Treasury from all sources during the fiscal year ending June 30, 1859, including the loan authorized by the act of June 14, 1858, and the issues of Treasury notes authorized by existing laws, were $81,692,471.01, which sum, with the balance of $6,398,316.10 remaining in the Treasury at the commencement of that fiscal year, made an aggregate for the service of the year of $88,090,787.11.

The public expenditures during the fiscal year ending June 30, 1859, amounted to $83,751,511.57. Of this sum $17,405,285.44 were applied to the payment of interest on the public debt and the redemption of the issues of Treasury notes. The expenditures for all other branches of the public service during that fiscal year were therefore $66,346,226.13. The balance remaining in the Treasury on the 1st July, 1859, being the commencement of the present fiscal year, was $4,339,275.54. The receipts into the Treasury during the first quarter of the present fiscal year, commencing July 1, 1859, were $20,618,865.85. Of this amount $3,821,300 was received on account of the loan and the issue of Treasury notes, the amount of $16,797,565.85 having been received during the quarter from the ordinary sources of public revenue. The estimated receipts for the remaining three quarters of the present fiscal year, to June 30, 1860, are $50,426,400. Of this amount it is estimated that $5,756,400 will be received for Treasury notes which may be reissued under the fifth section of the act of 3d March last, and $1,170,000 on account of the loan authorized by the act of June 14, 1858, making $6,926,400 from these extraordinary sources, and $43,500,000 from the ordinary sources of the public revenue, making an aggregate, with the balance in the Treasury on the 1st July, 1859, of $75,384,541.89 for the estimated means of the present fiscal year, ending June 30, 1860.

The expenditures during the first quarter of the present fiscal year were $20,007,174.76. Four million six hundred and sixty-four thousand three hundred and sixty-six dollars and seventy-six cents of this sum were applied to the payment of interest on the public debt and the redemption of the issues of Treasury notes, and the remainder, being $15,342,808, were applied to ordinary expenditures during the quarter. The estimated expenditures during the remaining three quarters, to June 30, 1860, are $40,995,558.23, of which sum $2,886,621.34 are estimated for the interest on the public debt. The ascertained and estimated expenditures for the fiscal year ending June 30, 1860, on account of the public debt are accordingly $7,550,988.10, and for the ordinary expenditures of the Government $53,451,744.89, making an aggregate of $61,002,732.99, leaving an estimated balance in the Treasury on June 30, 1860, of $14,381,808.40.

The estimated receipts during the next fiscal year, ending June 30, 1861, are $66,225,000, which, with the balance estimated, as before stated, as remaining in the Treasury on the 30th June, 1860, will make an aggregate for the service of the next fiscal year of $80,606,808.40.

The estimated expenditures during the next fiscal year, ending 30th June, 1861, are $66,714,928.79. Of this amount $3,386,621.34 will be required to pay the interest on the public debt, leaving the sum of $63,328,307.45 for the estimated ordinary expenditures during the fiscal year ending 30th June, 1861. Upon these estimates a balance will be left in the Treasury on the 30th June, 1861, of $13,891,879.61. But this balance, as well as that estimated to remain in the Treasury on the 1st July, 1860, will be reduced by such appropriations as shall be made by law to carry into effect certain Indian treaties during the present fiscal year, asked for by the Secretary of the Interior, to the amount of $539,350; and upon the estimates of the postmaster-General for the service of his Department the last fiscal year, ending 30th June, 1859, amounting to $4,296,009, together with the further estimate of that officer for the service of the present fiscal year, ending 30th June, 1860, being $5,526,324, making an aggregate of $10,361,683.

Should these appropriations be made as requested by the proper Departments, the balance in the Treasury on the 30th June, 1861, will not, it is estimated, exceed $3,530,196.61.

I transmit herewith the reports of the Secretaries of War, of the Navy, of the Interior, and of the postmaster-General. They each contain valuable information and important recommendations well worthy of the serious consideration of Congress. It will appear from the report of the Secretary of War that the Army expenditures have been materially reduced by a system of rigid economy, which in his opinion offers every guaranty that the reduction will be permanent. The estimates of the Department for the next have been reduced nearly $2,000,000 below the estimates for the present fiscal year and $500,000 below the amount granted for this year at the last session of Congress.

The expenditures of the Post-Office Department during the past fiscal year, ending on the 30th June, 1859, exclusive of payments for mail service specially provided for by Congress out of the general Treasury, amounted to $14,964,493.33 and its receipts to $7,968,484.07, showing a deficiency to be supplied from the Treasury of $6,996,009.26, against $5,235,677.15 for the year ending 30th June, 1858. The increased cost of transportation, growing out of the expansion of the service required by Congress, explains this rapid augmentation of the expenditures. It is gratifying, however, to observe an increase of receipts for the year ending on the 30th of June, 1859, equal to $481,691.21 compared with those in the year ending on the 30th June, 1858.

It is estimated that the deficiency for the current fiscal year will be $5,988,424.04, but that for the year ending 30th June, 1861, it will not exceed $1,342,473.90 should Congress adopt the measures of reform proposed and urged by the Postmaster-General. Since the month of March retrenchments have been made in the expenditures amounting to $1,826,471 annually, which, however, did not take effect until after the commencement of the present fiscal year. The period seems to have arrived for determining the question whether this Department shall become a permanent and ever-increasing charge upon the Treasury, or shall be permitted to resume the self-sustaining policy which had so long controlled its administration. The course of legislation recommended by the Postmaster-General for the relief of the Department from its present embarrassments and for restoring it to its original independence is deserving of your early and earnest consideration.

In conclusion I would again commend to the just liberality of Congress the local interests of the District of Columbia. Surely the city bearing the name of Washington, and destined, I trust, for ages to be the capital of our united, free, and prosperous Confederacy, has strong claims on our favorable regard.

www.ingramcontent.com/pod-product-compliance
Lightning Source LLC
Chambersburg PA
CBHW070528290526
45790CB00003B/1347